WISDOM

— FOR —

DAD

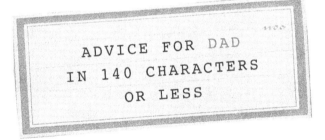

ADVICE FOR DAD
IN 140 CHARACTERS
OR LESS

WITH TWEETS FROM

DUDE
TO DAD

OTHERS

Published by Familius™ LLC, www.familius.com

Familius books are available at special discounts for bulk purchases for sales promotions, family or corporate use. Special editions, including personalized covers, excerpts of existing books, or books with corporate logos, can be created in large quantities for special needs. For more information, contact Premium Sales at 559-876-2170 or email specialmarkets@familius.com.

Library of Congress Catalog-in-Publication Data

2014935352

pISBN 978-1-939629-95-1

eISBN 978-1-939629-42-5

Printed in the United States of America

Edited by Maggie Wickes

Book and cover design by David Miles

Author photo by Abby Bischoff

10 9 8 7 6 5 4 3 2 1

First Edition

DEDICATED

to Jim Draplin, who on the night we met said,
"Spend more time with your kids when they're
young." #Dedicated #WisdomForDad

And, to Scott Friesen, who let me sit in the
front row and watch as he learned the ropes of
fatherhood (and played hours of video games).
#Dedicated

Finally, to Chris Lien, who led me through the
early parts of D2D transition with wisdom,
patience, and the love he shows Annie.
#Dedicated

ACKNOWLEDGMENTS

Thanks to @MikeBilleter, who is a world-class editor and the kind of friend that every dad needs. Thanks for your friendship and your words. #Thanks

My beautiful and patient wife, @AmyHydeWeber, meets the world with a pure heart and a real sense of true north. I love her beyond words. #Thanks

All of my hopes, dreams, and love to @EmersonWeber and @FinianWeber. You represent the best of your mom and me. I adore you both. #Thanks

To @JimRWeber and @NancyLWeber, thanks for life, patience and grace. You've been exemplary role models and are even better grandparents. #Thanks

Thanks to the team of editors, designers, and visionaries @FamiliusTalk. You took a chance on me and gave me voice. Thanks, thanks, thanks. #Thanks

To the 85,000+ dudes, dads, granddads, and dad supporters that have followed @DudeToDad and this adventure. You are the reason I tweet! #Thanks

To the "and other dads" that helped make this book happen, you are heroes! Thanks for sharing your advice with the next generation of dads! #Thanks

And to my friend and sounding board, @AbbyBischoff, all I have to say is, "#YOLO." And, #Thanks.

When writing a book called *Wisdom for Dad*, it's important to acknowledge that all of your wisdom comes from mistakes made. #Acknowledgment

Dear Reader,

This book was written on Twitter via @DudeToDad. Tweets submitted by Dude to Dad members are credited to the original dads. The rest are hard-won wisdom directly from @HughWeber. Enjoy.

PART I

WISDOM

The idea that I would write a book called *Wisdom for Dad* must be among the most unlikely—and hilarious—occurrences in literary history. This is like Einstein writing an *Idiot's Guide* to anything or Mrs. Dude writing a best-selling cookbook.

Yet, the dictionary defines wisdom as, "knowledge gained by having many experiences in life." And experiences I have in abundance.

I've been poked in the eye by an infant and seen my fair share of baby nuggets. I've had puke in my ears and been kneed in the groin more times than I can count.

In the wisdom I've gained through mistakes and missteps, I hope you find shortcuts to being the dad you hope to be. Or, at the very least, I hope you enjoy the read and pass it on to the next dude that needs it.

Y ou're not a temporary replacement for Mom. A dad doesn't babysit— he parents.

There is no line you cross when you know how to be a dad. Our children teach us how to become parents.

Jerry Nagel

It's smart to baby-proof the house. Just make sure you know how to lift the baby-proofed toilet seat before it's an emergency.

When my grandkids
want ice cream, I say
they can as soon as
they pick up all the
pine cones in my yard.
We're all happy!

ECONOMICS 101.

Ted Stephens

L ove and discipline are better together. Just like you and your bride.

@MindFlame

ur kids shouldn't have to wonder how we feel about them. Speak of your love for them often. Our words can give them life.

@adamweber

Social media has the potential to be a valuable parenting resource or a source of terrible advice. Find a community of value!

The biggest misconception that I had as a new dad was that I would somehow "figure out" or "fix" my kid.

THAT WAS SURE

Miss your days as a dude?

STOP.

The world has too many dudes. What the world *needs* is more dads. Focus on being a great one.

@MikeBilleter

The most valuable thing you own (laptop, heirloom vase, or JFK autograph) is now a target for destruction. You've been warned.

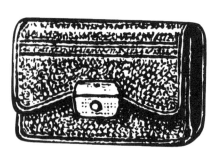

child is forced to operate in a world built for giants. Remembering this is a step toward understanding fear and insecurity.

As often as you think of it, look your children in the eyes and say, "I love you." You'll gain perspective, and so will they.

@zhamilton

hen your friends without kids try to tell you how to raise yours, forgive them. They know not what they do.

There's a fine line between behavior that is hilarious and behavior that needs to be corrected. Sometimes, the behavior is

BOTH.

R ewarding truth rather than punishing dishonesty leads to the desire to tell the truth . . . even if the truth hurts.

@cowboytweeter

S tore spare diapers in every open nook and cranny. The first day you don't have a spare and need one will be the worst day. Ever.

Your child owns you and you know it. And you're proud of it.

@QueenCityBakery

Baby books, with their "methods" and "milestones," are The Man's way of keeping you down. Don't let The Man keep you down.

THREE KEYS

for dadhood: Forgive.
Be purpose driven.
Serve your family.

@paterfamilius1

The way you were raised may have been successful, but so were covered wagons and horse-drawn carriages. Update accordingly.

You have no idea
what your patience or
tolerance is until you
have a child, and then
you learn it

QUICKLY.

@andrashewitt

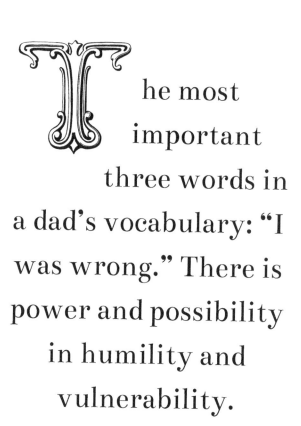

The most important three words in a dad's vocabulary: "I was wrong." There is power and possibility in humility and vulnerability.

Your kids will always prefer presence over presents.

Dads, here are three key things to do: be involved, be consistent, and love them for who they are.

THE REST WILL FOLLOW.

@Jeff48K

espite what pop culture may tell us about doofus dads, you're perfectly capable of parenting. Don't reinforce the stereotype.

The special little moments are gone before you know it. Take pictures and video often, but don't live behind your camera!

@genor03

I'm not sure who said, "Don't cry over spilled milk," but they clearly didn't see it happen six times in the same meal. Cry.

t's a beautiful day when you finally realize your kids are your teacher, not the other way around.

@joebart

The Beatles said, "All you need is love." I beg to differ. Every parent I know could also use some sleep and a bit of alone time.

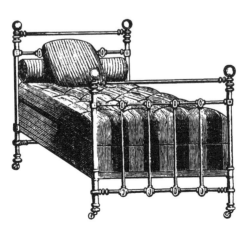

Imagine the worst
thing a child
could possibly do to
you. Multiply it by
ten. Expect it to
happen each and
every week.

You think this stage is the best? The worst? Give it a week and it's all bound to change again.

LEARN TO

LOVE THE

CURVEBALLS.

dults make poor
decisions
all the time.
Don't hold your kids
to a higher standard
than yourself.

@andytraub

I t seems that every family has a crazy aunt or uncle to provide a frame of reference for how good your parenting actually is.

You're never truly *ready* to be a dad—you simply run out of time to prepare. So when that baby arrives, be in it to win it!

DON'T

be so stressed about trying to teach your children everything. They will teach *you* more than you could ever imagine.

@tcollins

Before you were a
PARENT,
you were a
PARTNER.
Neglecting either is
bad for the other.

This thing we call life is highly improbable and extremely delicate. Don't take the life you created for granted.

You won't be patient with your kids if you are in HALT mode:

HUNGRY,

ANGRY,

LONELY,

TIRED.

@andytraub

abies pick up on feelings of stress in the household. This only makes parenthood even *more* stressful. So,

CHILL OUT.

SHOW

them that you value
their mother as an
equal, no matter your
situation.

@cowboytweeter

I suggest finding a dad that's a stage ahead, a dude that's a stage behind, and a dad in the same place. Triangulate for wisdom.

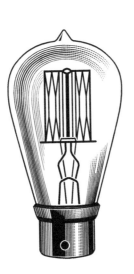

No matter what
mistakes you make
today,

TOMORROW

brings a new chance
to be the best dad you
can be.

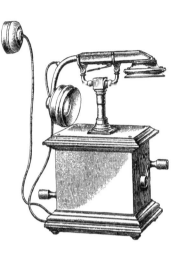

Make it a rule to avoid your phone when playing with your baby. Email can wait until naptime.

@chrismorello

You can try to fight the urge, but you will inevitably attempt to show pictures of your child to every human on earth.

The mother of *your* child? I haven't met her. But even I know that all she really wants is to be heard. So,

LISTEN TO HER.

aming your kid after a loved one is fine, but don't forget that Cornelius and Gertrude are still hefty names for six-year-olds.

L isten to "Cats in the Cradle." Cry. Learn. Then make time for your baby as much as you can . . . because they grow up.

@chrismorello

Becoming a dad
can be like a reset
button in

LIFE.

Use it as an
opportunity to
change your own
life for the better.

Find yourself a dude wingman. He'll remind you what it was like before kids and help you realize that you can't go back.

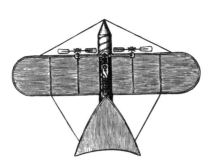

Kids will pick up your best traits and your worst habits. Always watch your words and your actions.

@BriAlNews

Everything changed
the moment you
became a dad. It's
neither good nor bad.

IT
JUST
IS.

The moment you realize you'll never fully catch up can either be demoralizing or liberating, but at least you get to choose.

stablish a bedtime routine! Go through the checklist with your kiddos every night until memorized! Smooth Bedtime = Happy Dad!

@genor03

emember the joys and heartbreaks of your childhood? Get ready to go through them all over again with your kids (only worse!).

The best-laid schemes of mice and men often go awry—because kids are basically real-life gremlins. Never feed 'em after midnight.

You really don't
need to smell it to
know that it

STINKS.

Faith, family, work. Keep things in that order and you'll be an amazing dad (and husband, employee, etc.).

@PaulTenHaken

Sometimes your baby poops more, mid-diaper change. That's called double doodie. Get it?

You wouldn't
be a dad
without them.
They wouldn't be
alive without you.
Try to remember
that you're in this
TOGETHER.

First, God; second, wife; third, kids. Spend time with all of them, so there are no regrets for time lost. Rejoice in the small things!

@jimrweber

There will be a moment—it will come earlier than you expect—when you'll want to feed your kid to a wolverine.

DON'T DO IT.

D on't forget to capture your own thoughts along the way. Whether tweets or handwritten notes, these are instant heirlooms.

If you're married, you'll remember when you suddenly had "couple friends." Prepare for the beginning of "friends with kids."

ever punish kids out of anger. Always sleep on it, pray about it, and make sure your spouse agrees with you before acting.

@clixable

I'm going to go out on a limb and recommend buying your own "World's Greatest Dad" mug. You're going to need the encouragement.

Find a way to give
Mrs. Dude some time
off. You need the time
alone with your kid.
She needs the time

SPEAK CALMLY.

The more often you raise your voice, the less impact it has. Save it for when it matters most.

@clixable

It shouldn't have to be said, but it shouldn't be left unsaid: abuse of a physical or verbal variety is for

COWARDS.

here's no room for division between Mom and Dad. Discuss and disagree in private, but always support each other's decisions.

WATCH

your words in
front of your
kids . . . for you'll
soon watch them
from your kids.

@PJWenzel

Sometimes the best decision you can make is to ask for

HELP.

In the end, if you and everyone you love survived the day, it's probably a win. But, do better tomorrow.

You'll
never
regret
putting
down your
phone and
picking up
your child.

@awayken

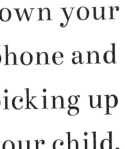

Sure, she's exhausted and possibly a real grump. However, it's also important to remember that she still probably LOVES you.

BEWARE THE IDES OF PRUNES.

@LarsLeafblad

PART II

WORK

Well-worn wisdom suggests that nobody on his deathbed says, "I wish I had spent more time in the office." While this may, in fact, be true, I might add that equally few people wish they had spent more time changing blow-out diapers, wrestling with a screaming, mid-tantrum toddler, or bathing in a warm mixture of spit-up and soggy crackers.

When it comes to the topic of work, the best we can do is to do our best. Don't let the digital world or electronic devices distract you from your child's ever-changing and evolving growth. At the same time, don't let the fear of missing out derail your professional productivity while you are working. The work-life balance on a day-by-day basis seems to be an elusive myth, but presence through our parenting lifetime is still very well within our reach.

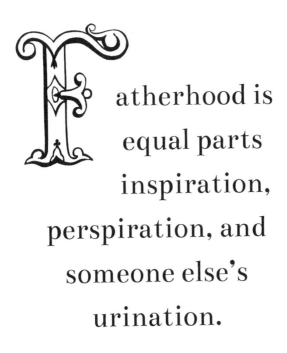

atherhood is equal parts inspiration, perspiration, and someone else's urination.

I've known some incredible fathers. But, I'm not them and none of them have experience with my wife or kids. Be your own expert!

One of the best
ways to help your
kids pursue their
dreams is to pursue
yours. It shows
them it's possible.

@JasonSalamun

There is no such thing as a perfect dad; just an average dude **DEDICATED** and **DETERMINED** to be the best dad he can possibly be.

Obsessing on your child's development is a bit like watching grass grow. Provide the necessary water and care, but don't hover.

tell my two sons I
love them every day.
I do not have a college
diploma, but I want
them to think I have a
doctorate in love.

@michaelburks79

I f you don't clean out the car seat every once in a while, your kid will. Usually by eating whatever he or she finds in it.

USUALLY

it's OK to trust your intuition. But it doesn't hurt to ask for a second opinion— especially if you haven't slept in days.

There are many definitions of

SUCCESS.

Make sure you're able to see your kids' definition, not only your own.

@SmoJump

You may never be as good as the dad that you put on a pedestal, but you can be the extraordinary dad your children deserve.

Help your kids develop a positive perception of work. Be careful how you talk about your job, even on the stressful weeks.

The most important work you can do is within the walls of your own

@paterfamilius1

Resilience, grit, and perseverance are worthy skills, but they are not learned through intimidation, manipulation, and control.

Don't outsource the important stuff. We're all busy, but doctor's appointments and school events are just too important to miss.

The simplest
of new learned
tasks inspire
the deepest of
prides.

@AndySBanks

Seek opportunities to engage and express yourself as a dad. Whether you're the photographer or a pretend horse,

BE YOU.

Long-term plans will often lead to disappointment for you or the little one. One week at a time is best—sometimes one day.

Y ou have the power to fix *everything*. It'll require some resourcefulness, but you are their Superhero. *Be* their Superhero.

@AmyHydeWeber

arenting is like running a marathon. You'll be exhausted. There will be puking. And chances are everything will smell funky.

Every kid is different.
What worked like
a charm for Kid
#1 might not be so
magical with Kid #2.
Adapt and adjust.

Parenting and success have the same secret: work hard and pivot around the unexpected.

@awayken

Think you've got parenting figured out? Have a second kid.

I DARE YOU.

Over the past fifty
years, parenting has
changed as much
as technology has.
Make sure you're
using an updated
manual.

Dads need to remember to teach their boys to be both tough and tender. One balances out the other.

@BriAlNews

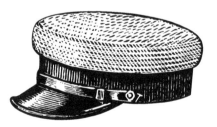

If your kid repeats things frequently, the problem may be in your lack of listening—not in their abundant

REPETITION.

Parenting with the heart of a learner and the spirit of an experienced guide assumes that children have something of value to share.

Washing bottles will
become the bane
of your existence
. . . but it'll score
you serious points
with the wife.
#ItsWorthIt

@IKnowJim

The idea of work-
life balance is a
myth. When you're
working, work.
When you're living,
live.

JUST BE

PRESENT

WHERE

YOU ARE!

The day your child is born, you'll be given an opportunity to be somebody's first hero. **MAKE THE MOST** of that opportunity.

"Since the day you were born, you were always____." Fill in the blank with your kid's greatness. Repeat often.

@MattPaese

For the first time in your life, someone else is completely dependent on you. Just know, failure really isn't an option.

Willpower
and patience
are limited-
but-renewable
resources. Cut
yourself a break
and take a mini-
sabbatical.
Seriously,

GO AWAY!

The most-uttered parent question, "How was your day?" must be abolished to really talk with kids. Share first. Ask later.

@MattPaese

Every morning, I make a decision to be a dad. It may sound ridiculous, but making the choice makes me responsible for the day.

When you reach
that place where
you think you can't
go any further,

DON'T.

Take a breath. Call
for reinforcements.
Get away.

utting
your
kids in
situations where
they could fail
helps them
realize how hard
they must work
to succeed.

@RyanSather

Parenting requires you to anticipate

FIVE MINUTES

from now and

FIFTY YEARS

from now. Both are important.

You'll be astounded
at how long you can
live in "survival
mode." Go ahead and
get comfy.

Set clear discipline boundaries and consistently enforce them (something I'm not very good at).

@SaffaZimbo

When the baby arrives, your wife doesn't need a pedestal. She needs a partner. A bit of pampering won't be discouraged though.

If you work full time, you'll have forty-eight hours or less with your kids each week.

MAKE THE MOST OF THE MOMENTS.

Teach your children to think critically and question everything— even you. And make them take debate; they will thank you.

@TravisDahle

I know you've got a lot on your plate as a new dad. But now is the time to start caring about education and savings.

Dads are a critical part of the parenting equation. Say it again: Dads are critical. Now,

EARN

IT.

B eing an awesome dad—if it were easy, everyone would be doing it.

@clreps

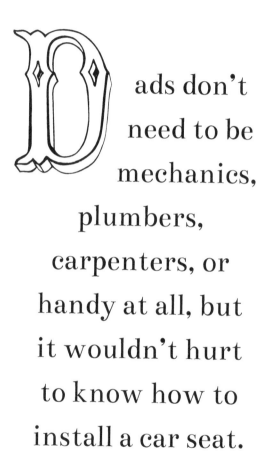

ads don't need to be mechanics, plumbers, carpenters, or handy at all, but it wouldn't hurt to know how to install a car seat.

Fatherhood is not a competitive sport. Treat it that way and you and your kids are likely to be miserable.

I never knew
parenting would
be this much
work. And I had
no idea it would be
this much fun.

@nathanschock

The best time to prepare to become a dad is before your kid is conceived. The second best time is

TODAY.

TEACH

them everything
you know and
know they heard
everything you
taught!

@Val_Lehnerd

Finding time for you may require getting up earlier in the morning or staying up later at night. Not easy, but important.

Find a hobby. Seriously. It doesn't matter if it's horseshoes or basket weaving. Just find something that's only for you.

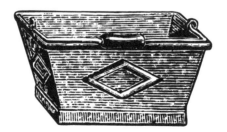

It turns out that
not being able to
breastfeed isn't a
sufficient excuse for
not helping at night.

WAKE UP!

PITCH IN!

ne of the best things you can do for your kids is offer them consistency. In schedule, expectations, and **LOVE.**

If you empower your
kids to make decisions
when you're around,
they'll be able to make
independent decisions
when you're not.

Ask your kids, ask yourself: "Did you ask any good questions today?"

@alexlundry

There are no "dad duties" or "mom duties" (except breastfeeding). Figure out where you can contribute best. Then,

JUMP IN.

When you say "no," make sure you mean "no." Once your kid realizes you'll budge with a tantrum or a threat, you're doomed.

It's OK to start out clueless about this whole adventure. It's not OK to stay that way.

PRACTICE,

PRACTICE,

PRACTICE.

you hand off the
baby every time he
or she cries, you'll
never develop
the bond that can
soothe them.

RUN

toward the wails.

PART III

PLAY

We knew how to play before we had the word to describe it. At the time, it may have seemed to be merely for enjoyment or recreation. But, in hindsight, this activity without boundaries was the practice of life. Through play, we tested our fears on a dirt bike or imagined ourselves as the future president. Half a day as a superhero and the other half as an auto mechanic? Don't mind if I do!

The freedom to run, paint, act, or dance seems to be the domain of children—but why? Why as dads can't we get down in the dirt? Why as adults can't we close our eyes and dream a bit? In the end, what's the worst that could happen? Perhaps a bit of whimsy and wasted time or, more likely, a deeper connection with our kids.

WORK

but always make time
for play.

@cc_chapman

Find a moment each
day to just observe
your kids. In each
sleeping breath or
unfiltered giggle is

PURE

MAGIC.

with the flow.
When you find a
roll of toilet paper
unwound, have a TP
fashion show.

@viasiouxfalls

Enjoy each day as a precious gift, new dads. In just

4,745

days, you'll have a teenager.

BE

prepared

to eat

standing

up. And

sleep

standing

up . . . that

too.

@clreps

Baths, books, and bedtime. These are the ingredients for a quality evening with the little one.

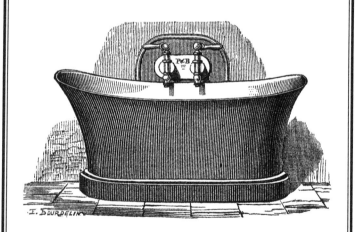

uture parents, want some practice? Wake up to death metal at 2 a.m. and try solving a calculus problem.

@Daddy_Lessons

149

Your child is a human garbage can. Their nose nuggets are probably the cleanest things they'll chew on today.

MOVE FORWARD.

R emoving yourself from a recently asleep baby is the closest you'll get to what it feels like to defuse a bomb.

@Daddy_Lessons

Some days will be filled with laughter. Other days will be filled with screaming and tears. Cherish the days with laughter.

When becoming a new dad, it's completely normal and socially acceptable to acquire a hazmat suit.

@JasonDKiner

Newborns are mobile. Pick them up and take them places. The different settings will stimulate them and remove your isolation.

When operating on boys, always use one of those wipes to cover Old Faithful, because his timing is unpredictable.

@jvervelde

At some point, at least one wall in your home will be covered in crayon/paint/marker. Try to appreciate the artistic intent.

The 3 Bs:

The primacy of reasons behind baby's sceams: Boobie (or bottle), Bowel Movement, and Boo Boo.

@viaSiouxFalls

Embrace your child's sense of wonder. You will be amazed at the places it can lead you.

What does your kid really want from you? My guess is they'd give up the video game or summer trip for more of your time.

At least

1/3

of becoming a truly
successful dad comes
down to mastering
a proper jig and one
funny voice.

Keep a good record of the noisy and messy toys your single friends give your kid. *THEIR* kids will love the same things one day.

Congrats on making it this far in life without someone throwing up in your ear, mouth, or hair. That streak is about to end.

Your kids will remind
you of who you
used to be as they
experience and learn
new things with eyes
wide open. #Play

@ToddLieman

I learned to put on diapers with a doll. It would have made more sense to use a professional wrestler or rabid squirrel.

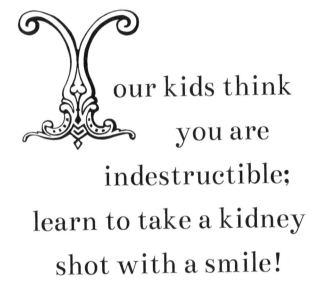

our kids think
you are
indestructible;
learn to take a kidney
shot with a smile!

@marconunezjr

They scream, you scream, we all scream . . . for no apparent reason. It does stop, and you should make sure you enjoy the quiet time.

The coolest sandbox in the world will sandblast your hardwood floors. What is outside will come inside,

EVERYWHERE.

@chadlockart

Be sure to capture the candid moments. These moments, which never appear in formal photographs, contain the best memories.

DON'T

be the first to comment on how rough or well the baby slept last night. You would be amazed at what I've slept through.

Luke Weber

Teach your kid one easy joke. Example: What did George Washington say to his men before they got in the boat? Get in the boat.

No one told me about this, so I'm telling you: at some point your kid's favorite word will be *penis.* Just roll with it.

@dawashington

The time will come when your child embarrasses you. Don't worry—you'll be able to embarrass him or her plenty in about 15 years.

Sing to them, have tea, and play babysitter. These moments will soon be long-ago memories.

@RyanMHall

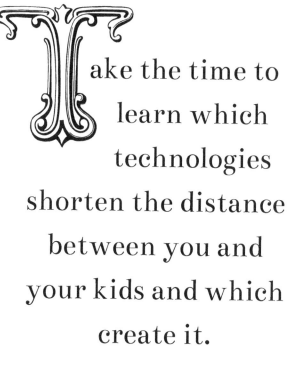

Take the time to learn which technologies shorten the distance between you and your kids and which create it.

Burping and farting are a baby's best friend, but hunger and fatigue are enemies to the end.

@the_rugby_coach

Remember when you were a kid and you felt disrespected, silenced, or belittled for being young?

DON'T DO

THAT TO

YOUR KID.

PARENTING

is easy until the baby
arrives.

@Daddy_Lessons

Kids are like a roller coaster with ups and downs, twists and turns, scary and joyful moments, all worthwhile—so buckle up.

Seth Honeyman

Lose your insecurities. Role model. Pay undivided attention. And get into Yo Gabba Gabba. #mutualdanceoff

@gbegin

Learn to celebrate tiny moments. Learning a new word deserves a party. Learning to use a toilet deserves a marching band.

Start watching shows like CSI or NCIS. This is a proper warm-up for the horror of your first up-the-back diaper blowout.

I wish I had recorded more of my daughter's voice early on. The joy she had as she began to discover language was amazing!

When holding baby playfully above your face right after he or she nursed, keep your mouth shut.

TIGHTLY.

@joebart

LIVE

for the giggle,
chuckle, and the all-
out laughter. They
will get you through
the gagging, choking,
and the all-out
disgusting.

R ead. With your kids, to your kids, and in front of your kids. Few skills are as significant as literacy and a love for learning.

K ids say the darndest things to share in Facebook status updates.

@LarsLeafblad

"Go play outside" shouldn't be a command strictly reserved for your children. Get outside and enjoy nature with them.

If given the option of the infant poking you in the eye with their finger or the 4-year-old kneeing you in the groin,

RUN.

on't
sweat
your
embarrassing
moments—they're
the ones your kids
will remember most
affectionately years
later.

njoy each
and every
moment,
because
before you know it,
the moments turn
into days, months,
and years.

@slobotski

In thirty years, you won't look back and think you took too many photos. It's more likely that you'll wish you would've taken more.

B uy some slippers. They may make you look tragically unhip, but they'll save your feet from Legos and other land mines.

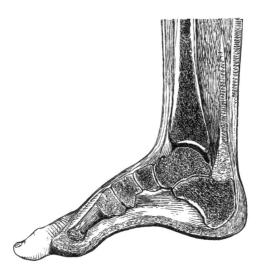

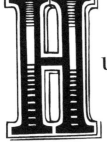ug, snuggle, and kiss. Your wife and your kids. Positive physical touch is critical from infancy to adulthood.

PART IV

DO
GOOD

ecent research has shown that doing good is contagious. You read that right. Just by giving charitably to a cause, volunteering in your community, or supporting others publicly, you can influence not only the people that you know, but also many of the people that they know. Your acts of good can result in an increased chance of good being done by your kids, their friends and even their friends' friends. What an opportunity to make an impact!

And, doing good doesn't require deep pockets or daily volunteering. The truth is, all it may require is a willing smile and an optimistic outlook. In fact, that same research has shown that happiness can be viral as well. That's right, just by being happy you can influence your network's happiness. And, if spreading happiness isn't doing good, I don't know what is.

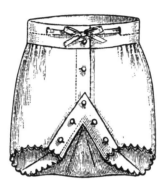

Try to be a proactive rather than a reactive dad. Don't know the difference? Proactive: diaper change. Reactive: diaper blowout.

TOUCH

is a powerful bonding
tool for families.
We've instituted a
daily thirty-second
hug in our house. Let
the endorphins flow!

Tell your kids you love them every day. Then make sure your actions match your words.

@nathanschock

Being a dad isn't about wearing Cosby sweaters or always having the answers. It's about creating a safe, loving home for kids.

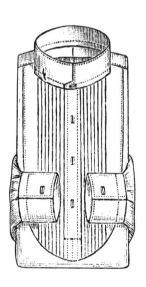

ust as much as your children need to hear "I love you," they need to hear "I'm here for you," as well.

You don't need many friends, but treat the really close ones like gold. They are more important than you can ever imagine.

@cc_chapman

Be the person around
your kids that you
want them to be when
they grow up.

@TheLaidBackDad

The first year has its challenges, but when your baby smiles, your heart melts, your priorities focus, and your life is better.

@PhillipStutts

There is plenty of bad on display at every turn, so there's no need to spotlight it.

POINT OUT THE GOOD INSTEAD!

You're going to fail. Learn to fail fast. Be sure to correct, adapt, or apologize immediately and then move

FORWARD.

When your kids are about to do something you think is risky, it's better to tell them to "pay attention" vs. "be careful."

@jtwinsor

When you think about your kids and find yourself smiling, you're doing a good job!

@MikeBySmith

There's a moment as kids fall asleep where their bodies go limp. This is the infant version of a trust fall.

DON'T DROP THEM.

TALK

to kids with the
respect you'd give
a friend, and the
likelihood that
they return that
respect is increased
dramatically.

There's often a fine line between a piece of chocolate and a baby nugget. My advice: don't make a guess in the dark.

No two kids are
alikc, so fight
off that urge to
compare yours
to that neighbor
kid who won
the spelling bee
at age three.

SHARE
GRATITUDE..

My daughter and I
end almost every day
sharing three things
we're grateful for.
It's the best part of
my day.

MODEL

generosity for your child.

ALTRUISM

and

PHILANTHROPY

are infectious. And generous hearts are happy hearts.

When I'm up all night with a sleepless kid, I like to whisper, "You're loved." It's better than the alternatives at 3:00 a.m.

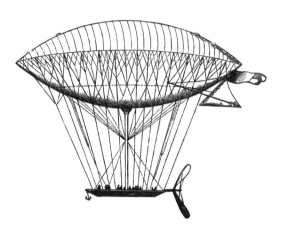

We should always share our dreams with our kids, but be careful not to project our dreams onto our kids.

TIME

away from your kids is inevitable. Use this time to refresh and renew, not to beat yourself up for being absent.

If you have to choose between being

KIND

and being

RIGHT,

choose being

KIND

and you will always be

RIGHT.

@QueenCityBakery

In most cases, the gift of experiences will last longer than the gift of things.

FIND TIME

to communicate with the people that matter to you. They help to remind you who you are as a dad and as a human being.

SUCCESS IN

PARENTING IS

NOT ABOUT

PERFECTION.

IT'S ABOUT

GETTING BETTER

EACH DAY.

Kids repeat everything they hear. Think about that before you fire up your "Hardcore Gangsta Rap" playlist, Big Poppa.

Your wife is a mom now. Much like you, she's crossed over and can't go back. Extend grace as she figures out the new normal.

No matter how hard things get with kids, there is

ALWAYS

something to be thankful for;

FIND IT.

@thehilker

Helping your children become the best possible version of themselves should be your greatest ambition as a parent.

Praise your child with "You did it!" rather than "Good job." It's much more meaningful and establishes independence!

Spend time with your kids doing "their things" and also "your things." It'll build strong, reciprocal relationships.

You have the power to influence all of your child's perspectives and prejudices. Will you use your powers for good?

ALWAYS

remember they are watching. Even when you don't think they are.

@wschlotter

Stop keeping track
of your failures—
those will pile up way
too quickly. Instead,

CELEBRATE

THE

SUCCESSES.

LET YOUR

CHILD SHOW

YOU WHO THEY

REALLY ARE.

DON'T PROJECT

ONTO THEM

WHO YOU HOPE

THEY'LL BE.

You either leave a legacy of abundance or scarcity for your children.

CHOOSE

ABUNDANCE.

In generosity, in praise, and in love.

No matter what crazy things your kids may do, remember that they're still learning. Keep that in mind for yourself as well.

Be open to big questions and even more open to big answers. How you respond early on will impact communications when it matters.

MOM

cries for attention
as much as the kids
do. It's just not as
obvious.

@rosmanfam

YOU HAVE THE POWER

to demonstrate for your son how to be a husband and for your daughter how to choose one. Don't mess this up.

Be clear, calm, and consistent. Talk with, not at, your kids. Laugh daily. Love and respect your wife. Pray—a lot.

@davehaan1

CONTRIBUTORS

Brian Allen @BriAlNews

Andy Banks @AndySBanks

Joe Bartmann @joebart

Gene Begin @gbegin

Mike Billeter @MikeBilleter

Jim Braunschweig @IKnowJim

Michael Burks @michaelburks79

Conor Callahan @clreps

CC Chapman @cc_chapman

Trent Collins @tcollins

Hector Cruz @Daddy_Lessons

Travis Dahle @TravisDahle

Jason Ellsmere @TheLaidBackDad

Scott Friesen @SmoJump

Dave Haan @davehaan1

Ryan Hall @RyanMHall

Zachary Hamilton @zhamilton

Mark Henderson @clixable

Andrew Hewitt @andrashewitt

Tyler Hilker @thehilker

Seth Honeyman

Mitch Jackson @QueenCityBakery

Jason Kiner @JasonDKiner

Jeff Kirk @Jeff48K

Lars Leafblad @LarsLeafblad

Val Lehnerd @Val_Lehnerd

Todd Lieman @ToddLieman

Chad Lockart @chadlockart

Alex Lundry @alexlundry

Chris Morello @chrismorello

Jerry Nagel

Marco Nunez @marconunezjr

Matt Paese @MattPaese

Chad Pickard @cpinkdot

Miles Raasch @awayken

Eric Raasch @MindFlame

Christopher Robbins @paterfamilius1

Geno Rodriguez @genor03

Adam Rosman @rosmanfam

Jason Salamun @JasonSalamun

Josh Sapienza @viasiouxfalls

Ryan Sather @RyanSather

Billy Schlotter @wschlotter

Nathan Schock @nathanschock

Jeff Slobotski @slobotski

Michael Byron Smith @MikeBySmith

Ted Stephens

Phillip Stutts @PhillipStutts

Paul Ten Haken @PaulTenHaken

Andy Traub @andytraub

Jamin Ver Velde @jvervelde

Dominick Washington @dawashington

Adam Weber @adamweber

Amy Weber @AmyHydeWeber

Jim Weber @jimrweber

Luke Weber

PJ Wenzel @PJWenzel

Casey Wilson @cowboytweeter

John Winsor @jtwinsor

Josh Young @the_rugby_coach

Saffa Zimbo @SaffaZimbo

ABOUT DUDE TO DAD

Hugh Weber started DudetoDad.com as a genuine cry for help
from an ordinary dude who wanted to be an extraordinary dad.
He is the author of Amazon.com Parenting Bestseller, *Dude to
Dad: The First Nine Months*. He recently spoke at TEDxFargo
about his ongoing experiment to raise a "child of possibility"
and regularly speaks to groups about lessons learned as a dad.
Hugh is currently in the fifth year of his Dude to Dad transition
and lives in the OTA states with Mrs. Dude, his daughter
Emerson, and his son Finn.

ABOUT FAMILIUS

Welcome to a place where mothers are celebrated, not compared. Where heart is at the center of our families, and family at the center of our homes. Where boo boos are still kissed, cake beaters are still licked, and mistakes are still okay. Welcome to a place where books—and family—are beautiful. Familius: a book publisher dedicated to helping families be happy.

VISIT OUR WEBSITE: WWW.FAMILIUS.COM

Our website is a different kind of place. Get inspired, read articles, discover books, watch videos, connect with our family experts, download books and apps and audiobooks, and along the way, discover how values and happy family life go together.

JOIN OUR FAMILY

There are lots of ways to connect with us! Subscribe to our newsletters at www.familius.com to receive uplifting daily inspiration, essays from our Pater Familius, a free ebook every month, and the first word on special discounts and Familius news.

BECOME AN EXPERT

Familius authors and other established writers interested in helping families be happy are invited to join our family and contribute online content. If you have something important to say on the family, join our expert community by applying at:

www.familius.com/apply-to-become-a-familius-expert

GET BULK DISCOUNTS

If you feel a few friends and family might benefit from what you've read, let us know and we'll be happy to provide you with quantity discounts. Simply email us at specialorders@familius.com.

Website: www.familius.com

Facebook: www.facebook.com/paterfamilius

Twitter: @familiustalk, @paterfamilius1

Pinterest: www.pinterest.com/familius

The most important work

you ever do will be within the

walls of your own home.
